Coffee Lovers Coloring book ◖ for adults relaxation ◗

This wonderful and beautiful book for coffee lovers, takes you into the world of enjoyment and relaxation, through its coffee illustrations and coffee quotes …

There is nothing better and more beautiful than taking a cup of coffee and enjoying its taste, but the most wonderful is to drink it while you enjoy coloring this interesting book

Copyright © 2020 by Mar Ben

This coloring book
belongs to :

Coffee
BE STRONG
COFFEE IS FOR THE STRONG

Life
Life Begins
After Coffee

Black
Coffee
YES ! I LIKE A HOMEMADE COFFEE

COFFEE IS ALWAYS A GOOD IDEA

COFFEE IS LOVE

RIDING THE COFFEE WAVE

COFFEE IS NOT JUST A BEVERAGE

Coffee
Is
The
Black
Black
Black
New Black

COFFEE IS THE BEST QUOTES

You can't make
Everyone happy
You are not
Coffee

COFFEE IS ART

You
Can Do It.
Coffee

Good day start with
Coffee & You
Coffee And You

COFFEE
AND
SMILE

A Nice Time
To Enjoy
Coffee & Cake

Romantic
coffee

coffee
and
Friends
Make the perfect blend

COFFEE FOR SUCCESS
IDEA
BUSINESS
SUCCESS
STRATEGY
$

12
9
3
6
coffee
book
drink good
coffee
read good
books

Coffee is not just a drink
Coffee is not just a drink
Coffee is not just a drink
Coffee is not just a drink

I love the smell of
coffee in the morning

Wake up
with a
Cup of
Coffee

Magical
coffee

Coffee and Sea
Coffee

Coffee is the best hot drink

Coffee is a hug in a mug
Hug in a Mug

Coffee
Tea
Coffee and Tea...
Friends Forever

DRINK COFFEE
WITH
STRAW
A NEW
STYLE

COFFEE
IS FOR
WINNERS

HOME IS WHERE THE COFFEE IS

We hope you enjoyed this coloring
book and had a good time
coloring it

Thank you